DISCOVER SERIES
BUNNY & PUPPY

SPANISH Bilingual EDITION

CONEJITO Y PERRITO

Perrito y Conijito Enojado

Angry Puppy and Bunny

Perrito y Conejito se colocan para una foto torpe

Puppy and Bunny pose for an awkward picture

Almohada de Conejito

Bunny Pillow

Conejito se acurruca sobre Perrito

Bunny rubs up against Puppy

Amor Conejito y Perrito

Love Bunny and Puppy

Perrito y Conejito se enfrentan

Puppy and Bunny face off

Perrito besa a conejito

Puppy kisses a bunny

Perrito lame al conejito

Puppy licks the bunny

Conejito y Perrito tocan sus narices

Bunny and Puppy go nose to nose

Perrito acaricia al conejito

Puppy nuzzles a bunny

Conejito hace una buena almohada

Bunny makes a good pillow

Conejito y Perrito se colocan para una foto

Bunny and Puppy pose for a picture

Conejito y perrito largo listos para acurrucarse

Bunny and long puppy get ready to snuggle

Pasear el Conejito

Ride the Bunny

Perrito huele el Conejito

Puppy sniffs the bunny

Oler antes de lamer

The sniff before the lick

Perrito huele el Conejito

Puppy sniffs Bunny

Perrito se acurruca a conejito

Puppy snuggles a bunny

Perrito pasa sobre Conejito

Puppy steps over Bunny

Conejito ataca a perrito

Bunny tackles a puppy

Perrito le da a Conejito un beso grande

Puppy give Bunny a big lick

Nos están mirando?

Are you looking at us?

Perrito más conejito más perrito es igual a tres

Puppy plus bunny plus puppy equals three

Dos perritos y un conejito

Two puppies and a bunny

Conejito y perrito te están mirando!

Bunny and puppy are looking at you!

Make Sure to Check Out the Other Discover Series Books from Xist Publishing:

Published in the United States by Xist Publishing
www.xistpublishing.com
PO Box 61593 Irvine, CA 92602

© 2017 First Bilingual Edition by Xist Publishing
Spanish Translation by Victor Santana
All rights reserved
No portion of this book may be reproduced without express permission of the publisher
All images licensed from Fotolia

ISBN: 978-1-53240-247-0 EISBN: 978-1-53240-246-3

xist Publishing